LUCA STEFANO CRISTINI

# FLOWERS, BUTTERFLIES, INSECTS, CATERPILLARS AND SERPENTS ...

## From Sybilla Merian & Moses Hariss XVII-XVIII Centuries engravings

### FIORI, FARFALLE, INSETTI, BRUCHI E SERPENTI ...
### DALLE SUPERBE INCISIONI DI SYBILLA MERIAN E MOSES HARISS

In those years, Europe was full of bonfirescommitted to make a clean sweep of witches. At the same time a young scientist: Sybilla Merian, daughter of the well-known German engraver Matthaeus Merian, was instead committed to studying, and illustrating the microscopic world of insects, caterpillars and butterfliesand the little bigger world of flowers, plants and animals.The wonderful metamorphosis of caterpillars was the basis of her best work: Metamorphosis Insectorum Surinamensium, published in Amsterdam in 1705. The work carried out by Sibylla Merian is fantastic. Indeed, during that time, it was unusual to deal with insects - the beasts of Satan. Her drawings of plants, snakes, spiders, iguanas and tropical beetles are still considered masterpieces and are sought-after by collectors around the world. Another great master, the English entomologist Moses Harris, contributed to complete the volume with his interesting engravings.

### DARWIN'S VIEW SERIES

Actually, the world from Darwin's point of view. The new series of Bookmoon specificallydedicated to the animal, vegetable and mineral world. A great review of nature through his most beautiful and fascinating images, taken from ancient tomes and essays about nature, made by the greatest individuals, artists and scientists together. Not only that, "Darwin's view" will involve yourself through the description of the stories, with facts and images of the exotic and romantic travels, made by the great explorers and brilliant scientists of the past, starting with the epic one on the HMS Beagle of our beloved and legendary Charles Robert Darwin!

I0081844

DARWIN'S VIEW

BOOKMOON
ARTE-STORIA-MUSICA

ISBN: 978-88-9327-084-7     2nd edition : May 2016

Title: Bookmoon Darwin's view 002 - **FLOWERS, BUTTERFLIES, INSECTS, CATERPILLARS & SERPENTS.... from Sybilla Merian & Moses Hariss XVII-XVIII centuries engravings** Serie realized by **Luca S. Cristini.** Editor: Soldiershop publishing. Cover & Art Design: Luca S. Cristini.

# FLOWERS, BUTTERFLIES, INSECTS, CATERPILLARS AND SERPENTS ...

Anna Maria Sibylla Merian nasce il 27 aprile del 1647 a Francoforte, un'anno prima della fine della guerra dei 30 anni. E' figlia del famoso incisore ed editore svizzero Matthäus Merian il vecchio (1593 - 1650), e di Johanna Sybilla Heim, sua seconda moglie. Il padre, già anziano muore quando Sibylla ha tre anni e la madre si risposa con Jakob Marell, pittore di fiori, che le insegnerà il disegno, la pittura ad olio, l'acquerello e l'incisione, arti che del resto fanno già parte del suo DNA artistico. Ha soli tredici anni quando inizia a dipingere insetti, piccoli animali e piante presi direttamente dalla sua osservazione diretta della natura. Nei suoi ricordi Sybilla parla dei bachi da seta, che per la prima volta osservo in filande presenti a Francoforte.

La giovane ragazza scopri presto che questi bachi, come altri bruchi, si trasformavano poi in belle farfalle, o falene notturne e diurne. Non solo ella si spinse a raccogliere tutti i bruchi che poteva trovare per osservarne la trasformazione. "Ma, per disegnarli e descriverli dal vero con tutti i loro colori, ho voluto esercitarmi anche nell'arte della pittura", dalla prefazione del suo celeberrimo Metamorphosis insectorum Surinamensium.

Nel 1665 la diciottenne Maria Sibylla Merian sposa il pittore quadraturista - specializzato in disegni prospettici di architetture - Johann Andreas Graff, allievo del patrigno, consolidando anor più, non ce b ne fosse bisogno, il suo humus artistico. Due anni dopo la copia si stabilisce a Norimberga. Nella città bavarese Sibylle inizia a studiare in maniera sempre più scientifica gli insetti e il ciclo vitale di bruchi e farfalle. Questa attività dimostra anche la forza e il grado di autonomia di questa scienziata. Occorre infatti ricordare che secondo le radicate opinioni del tempo, risalenti agli studi di Aristotele, gli insetti e le farafalle altro non erano che la risultante di una generazione spontanea avvenuta dalla putrefazione del fango e anche per questo gli insetti erano ritenuti dalla superstizione popolare vere e proprie bestie diaboliche.

▲ Ritratto della naturalista ed entomologa tedesco-olandese Maria Sibila Merian. Tela di Georg Gsell, circa 1710

*Portrait of German artist, scientist and entomologist Maria Sibylla Merian. Canvas of Georg Gsell. 1710 about.*

Maria Sibylla Merian was born on 2 April 1647 in Frankfurt, Germany, into the family of Swiss engraver and publisher Matthäus Merian the Elder. Her father died three years later and in 1651 her mother married still life painter Jacob Marrel. Marrel encouraged Merian to draw and paint. At the age of 13 she painted her first images of insects and plants from specimens she had captured. "In my youth, I spent my time investigating insects. At the beginning, I started with silk worms in my home town of Frankfurt. I realised that other caterpillars produced beautiful butterflies or moths, and that silk worms did the same. This led me to collect all the caterpillars I could find in order to see how they changed". (foreword from Metamorphosis insectorum Surinamensium — Metamorphosis of the Insects of Surinam)

In 1665 Merian married Marrell's apprentice, Johann Andreas Graff from Nuremberg; his father was a poet and director of the local high school, one of the leading schools in 17th century Germany. Two years later she had her first child, Johanna Helena, and the family moved to Nuremberg. While living there, Maria Sibylla continued painting, working on parchment and linens, and creating designs for embroidery patterns. She gave drawing lessons to unmarried daughters of wealthy patrician families (her "Jungferncompaney", i.e. virgin group), which helped the family financially, and increased their social standing. This provided her with access to the finest gardens, maintained by the wealthy and elite. Her first book, Neues Blumenbuch (New book of flowers) appeared in three parts in 1675-80. The drawings of single flowers or flower wreaths were to serve as patterns for amateur paintings or ladies needlework. The book continues a tradition of similar works from her father's (Merians) publishing house.

In those gardens, Merian began studying insects, particularly the lifecycle of caterpillars and butterflies. Many scholars of the time still believed that insects came from "spontaneous generation of rotting mud", an Aristotelian idea held in spite of—or perhaps because

Sybilla invece incuriosita, raccoglie questi bruchi e larve di insetti che porta nel suo laboratorio; nutrendoli e osservandone i comportamenti, scopre che essi nascano dalle uova e non dalla putrefazione di altre materie, che si racchiudono poi in un bozzolo dal quale escono trasformate in bellissime farfalle. Le disegna con rigore nei vari passaggi del loro sviluppo, quasi sempre in scenografia insieme con le piante sulle quali si situano abitualmente e delle quali si nutrono.

Questo vero lavoro certosino finisce, secondo la tradizione di famiglia nella stampa e pubblicazione dei suoi primi due libri: il primo viene edito nel 1675 con il titolo *Neues Blumenbuch* (Nuovo libro di fiori). A questo fa seguito, cinque anni dopo, una seconda edizione, in due volumi, intitolata *Florum fasciculi tres*. Questo secondo libro si basa su 36 tavole di incisioni colorate di fiori con una particolare e sofisticata cura di dettagli. Nel 1678 nasce la seconda figlia, Dorothea Henrica (1678 - 1745), che sposerà il pittore Georg Gsell (1673 – 1740) e diventerà la principale collaboratrice della madre. Nel 1679 Sibylla pubblica il suo secondo libro, *Der Raupen wunderbare Verwandlung und sonderbare Blumennahrung* (La meravigliosa metamorfosi dei bruchi e il loro singolare nutrirsi di fiori), di cui diamo qualche esempio a pag.10. Si tratta di una lavoro molto interessante ed innovativo dove sono illustrati gli stadi di sviluppo di 176 specie di farfalle e delle piante dei cui fiori esse si nutrono. Insieme alla tavola, l'anima naturalista di Sybilla riporta le sue osservazioni sulla vita di ogni insetto, con la minuziosa descrizione del processo di trasformazione. Nel 1685 si separa dal marito e parte col fratellastro Matthäus (1621 - 1687) e le due figlie per il castello Waltha in Olanda, andando a far parte di una comune protestante di labadisti, una setta pietista fondata dal francese Jean de Labadie; il castello era di proprietà di Cornelis van Sommelsdijk, allora governatore della colonia olandese del Suriname. E' proprio in questo castello che Sybilla entra in contatto per la prima volta con le farfalle tropicali, assai diverse da quelle alle quali lei è abituata. Nel castello infatti vi è conservata una collezione di farfalle tropicali provenienti appunto da questa lontana colonia olandese. Maria Sibylla tuttavia mal sopporta la rigida condotta di vita imposta alla comunità e lascia il castello nell'estate del 1691.

Va quindi a vivere ad Amsterdam: abitando in una casa che ben presto diventa un punto di incontro di naturalisti e collezionisti, dove stabilisce anche il suo

▲ **Altra incisione-**Ritratto di Maria Sibilla Merian. Stampa del XVIII secolo.

*Another engraving portrait of Maria Sibylla Merian. XVIII century.*

of—the teachings of the Catholic Church. Although St Thomas Aquinas concluded that spontaneous generation of insects was the work of the Devil, Pope Innocent V in the thirteenth century had declared that belief in spontaneous generation went against Church teachings, since all life was created in the first days of Creation chronicled in Genesis; however, the Greek tradition prevailed in parts of the scientific community. Francesco Redi is among the scientists who had shown that worms are born from eggs. Against the prevailing opinion, Merian studied what actually happened in the transformation of caterpillars into butterflies. She took note of the transformations, along with the details of the chrysalises and plants that they used to feed themselves; later, she collected all these sketches and illustrations of the stages of their development in her study book.

In 1678 her second daughter, Dorotha Maria (wife of painter Georg Gsell), was born, and one year later she published the first volume of her second book called Der Raupen wunderbare Verwandlung und sonderbare Blumennahrung -- The Caterpillar's Marvelous Transformation and Strange Floral Food. In this book she presented the stages of development of different species of butterflies along with the plants on which they fed. In the preface she asks the reader Suche demnach hierinnen nicht meine sondern allein Gottes Ehre Ihn als einen Schöpfer auch dieser Kleinsten und geringsten Würmlein zu preisen (Do not seek my glory herein but only God's to praise him as the creator also of these smallest and humblest worms). This labels the "caterpillar book" a book for meditation rather than a scientific book; it has to be seen in the tradition of seeking god in nature In 1681 Jacob Marrell died and the Graff family returned to Frankfurt in 1683 to handle the estate, including the house, art work, library and financial issues left unresolved at the time of his death. A lawsuit was filed by the fractured factions of the families. Upon its resolution in 1685, at the age of 38, Merian left her husband. Accompanied by her mother and daughters, she moved to the Labadist religious commune in Friesland,[3] who only accepted marriages between members of their community. The family moved into a home owned by Cornelis van Sommelsdijk, the governor of Surinam. Here she studied the world of South American tropical flora and fauna.

Five years later her mother died and she moved to Amsterdam. Merian's husband divorced her two years later, in 1692. In Amsterdam Merian and her

organizzato laboratorio e studio artistico. Il nuovo ambiente le risulta particolarmente stimolante, al punto da spingerla ad affrontare, insieme alla seconda figlia il periglioso viaggio, diventato ormai un sogno e un obiettivo, di raggiungere il Suriname olandese, posto dall'altra parte del globo.

Le difficoltà iniziano subito, dall'organizzazione del viaggio stesso. Questo è infatti assai rischioso e costoso, Sybilla non può contare su finanziamenti pubblici né privati, soprattutto a causa dello scetticismo con il quale questa inconsueta spedizione scientifica, condotta oltre tutto da donna viene considerata dalla gente.

La lungimiranza del borgomastro di Amsterdam le garantisce tuttavia l'assistenza della colonia e un prestito, che Maria Sibylla confida di poter restituire con i profitti che certo deriveranno dai frutti della spedizione, sotto forma di rari esemplari e soprattutto dalle vendite del nuovo libro che si propone di realizzare al suo ritorno.

Sibylla - che a ogni buon conto ha fatto testamento - parte da Amsterdam nel giugno del 1699 ed arriva 90 giorni dopo sulla costa del Suriname, stabilendosi a Paramaribo, capitale della colonia. L'intrepida donna si getta subito a capofitto nella sua impresa. Guidata da indio locali inizia esplorazioni di foreste poco accessibili e ricche di insidie; essi le mostreranno gli esemplari di piante, di fiori e di frutti, specie di insetti, di uccelli, di serpenti, di conchiglie. Sul posto l'animo curioso di Sybilla le allarga gli orizzonti.

Oltre a bruchi, farfalle, uova e insetti essiccati, raccoglie infatti anche uova di coccodrillo e di serpenti; essa li conserva nell'alcool o li fa essiccare, in vista del loro trasporto al ritorno in Olanda. Ovviamente la parte grafica continua a far la parte del leone, e Sybilla dipinge anche ananas, manioca, papate dolci, alberi dell'olio, papaia, e molte altre specie di frutti tipici della regione, insieme con animali come iguane, serpenti, lucertole, rane, coccodrilli, uccelli, ripromettendosi di rappresentarli insieme alle consuete immagini di piante e di insetti. Nel 1701 si ammala di febbre gialla ed è costretta a ritornare in Europa.

## La Metamorfosi degli insetti del Suriname

Quattro anni dopo il suo ritorno, finalmente esce ad Amsterdam il suo più famoso libro: *Metamorphosis insectorum Surinamensium*, che viene subito definita "l'opera più bella mai dipinta in America". Libro magnifico che le procura subito una meritata notorietà

▲ Frontespizio dell'opera di Sybilla Merian *Der Raupen wunderbare Verwandlung und sonderbare Blumennahrung* del 1679-1718.

*Frontispiece of the famous book of Sybilla Merian Der Raupen wunderbare Verwandlung und sonderbare Blumennahrung 1679-1718.*

work attracted the attention of various contemporary scientists. Her older daughter, Johanna Helena, married merchant Jacob Herolt, also a former member of the Labadists, and moved with him to Surinam, which was at that time a recently acquired Dutch colony.

In 1699 the city of Amsterdam sponsored Merian to travel to Surinam along with her younger daughter, Dorothea Maria. Before departing, she wrote:

In Holland, I noted with much astonishment what beautiful animals came from the East and West Indies. I was blessed with having been able to look at both the expensive collection of Doctor Nicolaas Witsen, mayor of Amsterdam and director of the East Indies society, and that of Mr. Jonas Witsen, secretary of Amsterdam. Moreover I also saw the collections of Mr. Fredericus Ruysch, doctor of medicine and professor of anatomy and botany, Mr. Livinus Vincent, and many other people. In these collections I had found innumerable other insects, but finally if here their origin and their reproduction is unknown, it begs the question as to how they transform, starting from caterpillars and chrysalises and so on. All this has, at the same time, led me to undertake a long dreamed of journey to Suriname. (foreword in Metamorphosis insectorum Surinamensium)

Merian worked in Surinam (which included what later became known as the French, Dutch and British Guianas) for two years,[3] travelling around the colony and sketching local animals and plants. She also criticized the way Dutch planters treated Amerindian and black slaves. She recorded local native names for the plants and described local uses. In 1701 malaria forced her to return to Netherlands. A painting showing the metamorphosis of Thysania agrippina produced in 1705. Another version exists in which all but the opened-winged butterfly is reversed. Back in the Netherlands she sold specimens she had collected and published a collection of engravings about the life in Surinam. In 1705 she published a book Metamorphosis Insectorum Surinamensium about the insects of Surinam.

In 1715 Merian suffered a stroke and was partially paralysed. She continued her work but the disease probably affected her ability to work; a later registry lists her as a pauper.

Maria Sibylla Merian died in Amsterdam on 13 January 1717. Her daughter Dorothea published Erucarum

fra i ceti più in alto nella società, tanta fatica tuttavia non bastò ancora a renderla completamente attendibile fra gli uomini di scienza, essendo il latino l'unica lingua accettata dalla comunità scientifica. I suoi disegni di piante, serpenti, ragni, iguane e coleotteri tropicali sono tuttora considerati dei capolavori e vengono ricercati dai collezionisti di tutto il mondo. Sofferente di cuore già dal 1711, Anna Maria Sibylla Merian muore d'infarto ad Amsterdam, settantenne, nel 1717.

## MOSES HARRIS

Mosè Harris è un noto entomologo Ed incisore britannico, nato nel 1731 e morto nel 1785. Si sa molto poco sulle sue origini, la sua educazione e la sua vita. Questo precoce interesse per la entomologia, probabilmente sotto l'influenza di uno dei suoi zii.
Harris è famoso per il suo libro, sistema naturale di Colori del 1766, basato sulle sue osservazione delle opere di Sir Isaac Newton. In campo entomologo invece la sua opera più famosa rimane *L'Aureliano*. In questo bellissimo trattato, che ricorda molto i lavori della Merian egli descrive 41 specie di farfalle, quattro scarabei e una libellula. Harris dedica ognuna delle su tavole ad una personalità nota , molto spesso si tratta di suoi collezionisti e ammiratori. Disegna gli insetti e gli animali descrivendo bene le diverse fasi del loro sviluppo. L'estetica delle sue tavole è innegabile e le sue opere, come già quelle di Sybilla Merian sono considerati tra le più riuscite del tempo. Pochi anni dopo, la prima pubblicazione esce l'Aureliano in formato economico, senza tavole. Egli vi descrive circa circa 400 specie britanniche. Dà ad ognuna di loro un nome in inglese, sempre accompagnato però dal corrispondente in latino secondo il sistema ufficiale in base alla 12a edizione del *Systema naturae*. Egli fu il primo naturalista a proporre lo studio delle nervature delle ali di farfalla per la loro classificazione nel suo saggio del 1767.
Harris ha prodotto illustrazioni di insetti per William Curtis (1746-1799) per la sua pubblicazione *The Botanical Magazine*, a William Martyn per il suo Nuovo Dizionario di Storia Naturale (1785) e, infine, a Dru Drury (1725-1804) per il primo volume di le sue illustrazioni di Storia Naturale (1770).

▲ **Autoritratto di Moses Harris,** illustre scienziato ed entomologo inglese. Vero erede dell'arte di Sybilla Merian.

*Selfportrait of the English scientist and entomologist Moses Harris.*

*Ortus Alimentum et Paradoxa Metamorphosis, a collection of her mother's work, posthumously.Merian worked as a botanic artist. She published three collections of engravings of plants in 1675, 1677 and 1680. Afterwards she studied insects, keeping her own live specimens, and made drawings showing insect metamorphosis, in which all life stages of the insect (egg, larva, pupa, and adult) were depicted in the same drawing. In her time, it was very unusual that someone would be genuinely interested in insects, which had a bad reputation and were colloquially called "beasts of the devil." As a consequence of their reputation, the metamorphosis of these animals was largely unknown. Merian described the life cycles of 186 insect species, amassing evidence that contradicted the contemporary notion that insects were "born of mud" by spontaneous generation. Moreover, although certain scholars were aware of the process of metamorphosis from the caterpillar to the butterfly, the majority of people did not understand the process.*

### MOSES HARRIS

*Moses Harris is a British entomologist and engraver, born in 1731 and died in 1785.We know only very little about his origins, his education and his life. This early interest in entomology, probably under the influence of one of his uncles. His most famous work is The Aurelian in which he describes forty-one species of butterfly, four beetles and dragonfly. Harris dedicates each board personality, probably one of his subscribers. He draws animals after living and often presents the different stages of development. The aesthetic is undeniable and his boards are considered among the most successful of the time. He published a few years later, an economical pocket, no illustration with the exception of an anatomical chart. He described about 400 species in Britain. It gives their name in English but also in Latin according to the Linnaean system based on the 12th edition of Systema naturae. He was the first naturalist to propose the use of the study ribs butterfly wings for their classification in his Essay of 1767.*

# THE PLATES
## LE TAVOLE

## ANNA MARIA SYBILLA MERIAN
### (1647-1717)
ENGRAVING FROM:
METAMORPHOSIS INSECTORUM SURINAMENSIUM, 1705
DER RAUPEN WUNDERBARE VERWANDLUNG UND
SONDERBARE BLUMENNAHRUNG 1679-1718
ERUCARUM ORTUS, ALIMENTUM ET PARADOXA
METAMORPHOSIS 1718

*Ananas Metamorphosis insectorum Surinamensium pl. 1 - Maria Sybilla Merian*

*Metamorphosis insectorum Surinamensium pl. 3 - Maria Sybilla Merian*

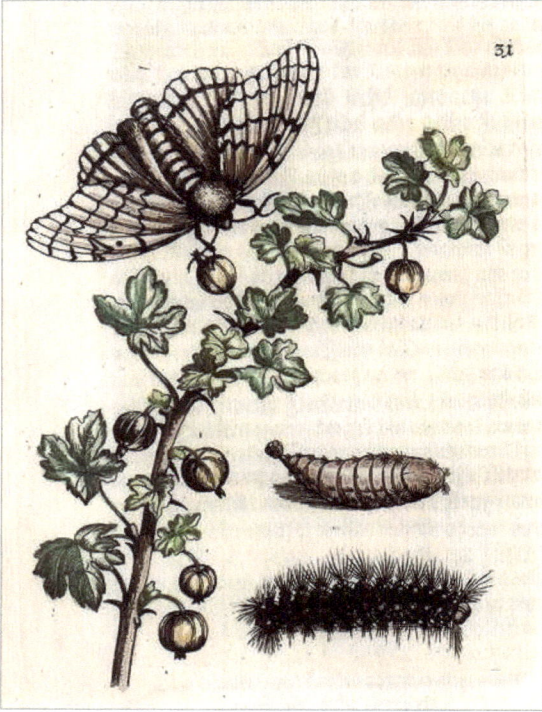

Tavole da Der Raupen WunderbareVerwandelung und Sonderbare Blumen-Nahrung - di Sybilla Merian

*Sauro e farfalle Metamorphosis insectorum Surinamensium pl. 4 - Maria Sybilla Merian*

*Metamorphosis insectorum Surinamensium pl. 5 - Maria Sybilla Merian*

*Metamorphosis insectorum Surinamensium pl. 7 - Maria Sybilla Merian*

*Metamorphosis insectorum Surinamensium pl. 8 - Maria Sybilla Merian*

*Metamorphosis insectorum Surinamensium pl. 11 - Maria Sybilla Merian*

*Banano Metamorphosis insectorum Surinamensium pl. 12 - Maria Sybilla Merian*

*Plum tree Metamorphosis insectorum Surinamensium pl. 13 - Maria Sybilla Merian*

*Annona muricata e falena Metamorphosis insectorum Surinamensium pl. 14 - M. S. Merian*

P. Sluyter Sculp.          Melon d'Eau

*Cocomero Metamorphosis insectorum Surinamensium pl. 15 - Maria Sybilla Merian*

*Metamorphosis insectorum Surinamensium pl. 16 - Maria Sybilla Merian*

*Tarantula Metamorphosis insectorum Surinamensium pl. 18 - Maria Sybilla Merian*

*Metamorphosis insectorum Surinamensium pl. 19 - Maria Sybilla Merian*

*Gumbo tree Metamorphosis insectorum Surinamensium pl. 20 - Maria Sybilla Merian*

*Amaryllis Metamorphosis insectorum Surinamensium pl. 22 - Maria Sybilla Merian*

*Banano e sauro Metamorphosis insectorum Surinamensium  pl. 23 - Maria Sybilla Merian*

*Metamorphosis insectorum Surinamensium pl. 24 - Maria Sybilla Merian*

*Metamorphosis insectorum Surinamensium pl. 26 - Maria Sybilla Merian*

*Mantide da Metamorphosis insectorum Surinamensium pl. 27 Maria Sybilla Merian*

*Metamorphosis insectorum Surinamensium pl. 29 - Maria Sybilla Merian*

*Metamorphosis insectorum Surinamensium pl. 30 - Maria Sybilla Merian*

*Fico Metamorphosis insectorum Surinamensium pl. 33 - Maria Sybilla Merian*

*Uva e falena Metamorphosis insectorum Surinamensium pl. 34 - Maria Sybilla Merian*

*Foglie di tabacco Metamorphosis insectorum Surinamensium pl. 36 - Maria Sybilla Merian*

*Metamorphosis insectorum Surinamensium pl. 38 - Maria Sybilla Merian*

*Patata dolce Metamorphosis insectorum Surinamensium pl. 41 - Maria Sybilla Merian*

*Metamorphosis insectorum Surinamensium pl. 43 - Maria Sybilla Merian*

*Metamorphosis insectorum Surinamensium pl. 46 - Maria Sybilla Merian*

*Metamorphosis insectorum Surinamensium pl. 47 - Maria Sybilla Merian*

*Metamorphosis insectorum Surinamensium pl. 48 - Maria Sybilla Merian*

*Metamorphosis insectorum Surinamensium pl. 49 - Maria Sybilla Merian*

*Metamorphosis insectorum Surinamensium pl. 51 - Maria Sybilla Merian*

*Metamorphosis insectorum Surinamensium pl. 53 - Maria Sybilla Merian*

*Red Ginger con ape Metamorphosis insectorum Surinamensium pl. 54 - Maria Sybilla Merian*

*Metamorphosis insectorum Surinamensium pl. 55 - Maria Sybilla Merian*

*Metamorphosis insectorum Surinamensium pl. 56 - Maria Sybilla Merian*

*Metamorphosis insectorum Surinamensium pl. 57 - Maria Sybilla Merian*

*Metamorphosis insectorum Surinamensium pl. 58 - Maria Sybilla Merian*

*Rana femmina Metamorphosis insectorum Surinamensium pl. 59 - Maria Sybilla Merian*

*Cardinal's Guard Metamorphosis insectorum Surinamensium pl. 60 - Maria Sybilla Merian*

# THE PLATES
## LE TAVOLE

## MOSES HARRIS
## (1730-1788)

### ENGRAVINGS FROM:
### THE AURELIAN OR NATURAL HISTORY OF ENGLISH INSECTS
### (1766)

Plate 1 from The Aurelian or natural history of English insects 1766 - Moses Harris

To the Right Hon.ble EARL BROOKE &c
His Lordships most

This Plate is Humbly Inscribed by
Obedient & Devoted Servant
Moses Harris.

*Plate 2 from The Aurelian or natural history of English insects 1766 - Moses Harris*

Pl. III.

Plate 3 from The Aurelian or natural history of English insects 1766 - Moses Harris

To his Grace Henry. Augustus Fitzroy. Duke of Grafton, Earl of Euston &c.
This Plate is most humbly Dedicated by his Graces most Obed.t & faithful Servant.
Moses Harris

Plate 4 from The Aurelian or natural history of English insects 1766 - Moses Harris

*Plate 5 from The Aurelian or natural history of English insects 1766 - Moses Harris*

Plate 7 from The Aurelian or natural history of English insects 1766 - Moses Harris

To Sir Henry Ecklin Baronet

This Plate is humbly Inscribed by his most Obliged & Obedient Servt Moses Harris

*Plate 8 from The Aurelian or natural history of English insects 1766 - Moses Harris*

To the Right Hon.*ble* Lord Viscount        Charlemont, this Plate is Humbly
Inscribed by his Lordships most        Obliged & Obedient Serv.*t* Moses Harris.

*Plate 9 from The Aurelian or natural history of English insects 1766 - Moses Harris*

To the R.t Hon.ble Lady Henrietta    *Alicia Wentworth*
This Plate is most humbly Dedicated    by her Ladyship's most obliged & obedient Serv.t
Moses Harris.

*Plate 10 from The Aurelian or natural history of English insects 1766 - Moses Harris*

To the R.t Hon.ble Lady Charlott
This Plate is most humbly Dedicated

Townshend Baroneſs Ferrers
by her Ladyships most obliged & faithful Serv.t
Moses Harris J.Gretton

Plate 11 from The Aurelian or natural history of English insects 1766 - Moses Harris

PL. XII

To the Right Honourable *Countess of Dalkeith*
This Plate is most humbly Dedicated by her Ladyships most Obliged & Obedient Serv.
Moses Harris

*Plate 12 from The Aurelian or natural history of English insects 1766 - Moses Harris*

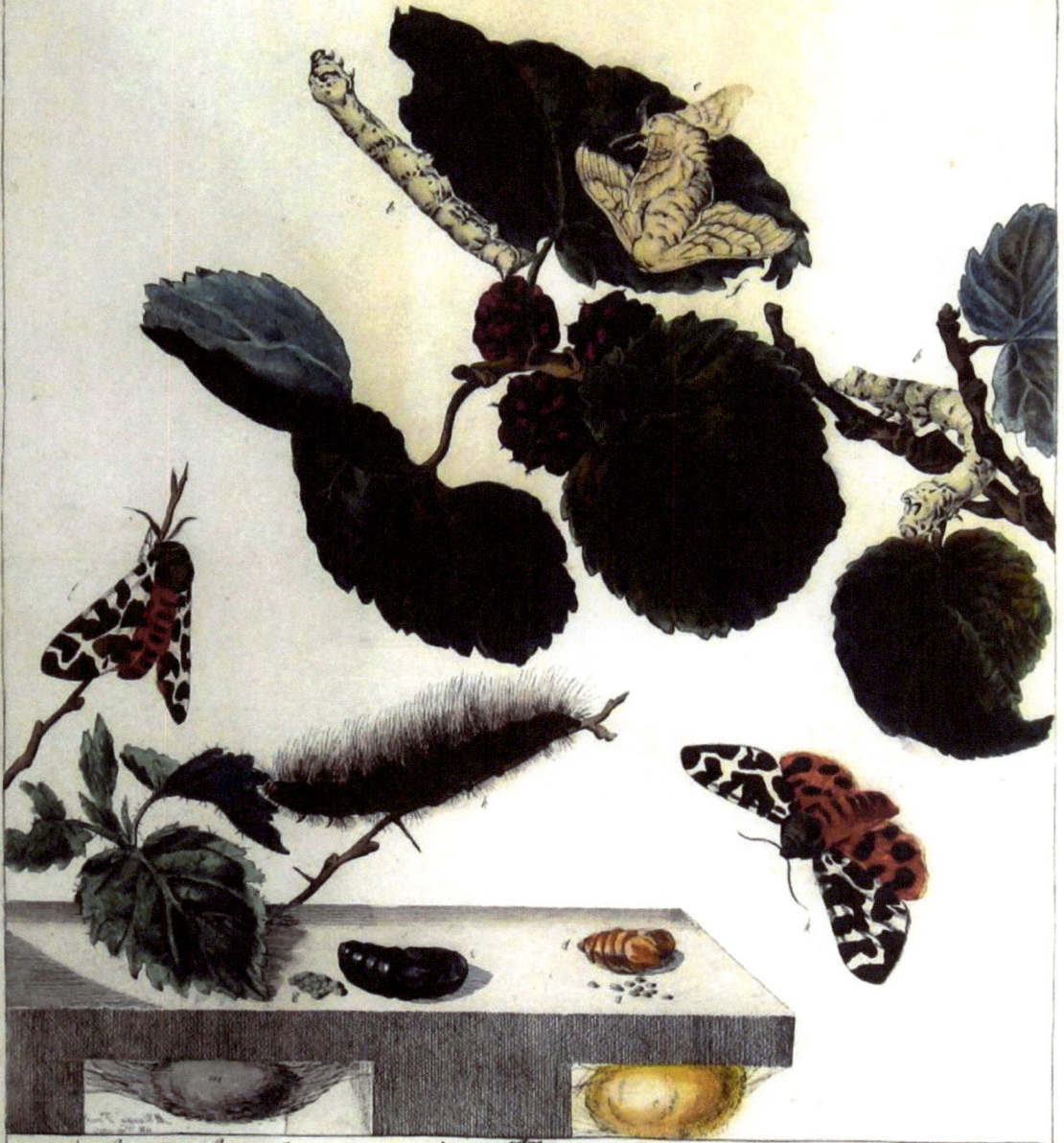

To the Right Honourable
This Plate is most humbly Dedicated

Countess of Ailesford
by her Ladyships most obliged & obedient Servt.
Moses Harris

Plate 13 from The Aurelian or natural history of English insects 1766 - Moses Harris

To the Right Honourable Countefs of Stamford
This Plate is humbly Dedicated by her Ladyships most Obedient & Faithful Serv.
Moses Harris.

Plate 15 from The Aurelian or natural history of English insects 1766 - Moses Harris

M.ʳHarris ad Vivum

To the Right Honourable Lady Carysfort, This Plate is Most Humbly Dedicated by her Ladyships most Obliged & Obed.ᵗ Humble Servant. Moses Harris

MANUS HÆC INIMICA TYRANNIS

Plate 17 from The Aurelian or natural history of English insects 1766 - Moses Harris

PL. XVIII.

*Plate 18 from The Aurelian or natural history of English insects 1766 - Moses Harris*

To Her Grace the Dutchess of Richmond.
This Plate is humbly Dedicated by her Graces most Oblig'd & Obed'. Hum:ble Serv'.
Moses Harris.

Plate 20 from The Aurelian or natural history of English insects 1766 - Moses Harris

*Plate 22 from The Aurelian or natural history of English insects 1766 - Moses Harris*

70

*To the R.t Hon.ble the Earl of Suffolk's*
*This Plate is most humbly Dedicated by his Lordship's most Obed.t Serv.t*
*NON QUO SED QUOMODO*
*Moses Harris.*

Plate 23 from The Aurelian or natural history of English insects 1766 - Moses Harris

To the Right Honourable the Countess of Berkeley
This Plate is humbly dedicated by her Ladyship's most Obedient Humble Servant Moses Harris.

Plate 25 from The Aurelian or natural history of English insects 1766 - Moses Harris

To the Rt. Hon.ble Lady Spencer this Plate is most humbly Dedicated by her Ladyship's most obliged humble Servant Moses Harris.

DIEU DEFEND DROIT

Plate 26 from The Aurelian or natural history of English insects 1766 - Moses Harris

To Her Grace the Dutchess of Norfolk
This Plate is humbly dedicated by Her Grace's most devote Servant,
Moses Harris.

*Plate 27 from The Aurelian or natural history of English insects 1766 - Moses Harris*

PL. XXXVI.

To the Rev.ᵈ Mʳ                    Willᵐ Ray
This Plate is humbly Dedicated          by his most humble Obliged Servᵗ
MOSES HARRIS

Plate 36 from The Aurelian or natural history of English insects 1766 - Moses Harris

N. Barris et Vivares Sculp.

To my Ingenous Friend and Benefactor Mr. Dru Drury
This Plate is most Humbly Dedicated by his Obliged Servant Moses Harris

Plate 37 from The Aurelian or natural history of English insects 1766 - Moses Harris

*Plate 38 from The Aurelian or natural history of English insects 1766 - Moses Harris*

Plate 42 from The Aurelian or natural history of English insects 1766 - Moses Harris

*Plate 44 from The Aurelian or natural history of English insects 1766 - Moses Harris*

# TITOLI PUBBLICATI - ALREADY PUBLISHING

Della stessa collana

**Aranci, mandarini, cedri limoni e bergamotti... Artistici agrumi dalle incisioni di Ferrari, Aldrovrandi, Volckhamer..**
Curiosa e attenta raccolta di immagini di esemplari botanici appartenenti alla famiglia degli agrumi realizzati da artisti scienziati, biologi e antropologi. Artisti del passato impegnati nella realizzazione di veri e propri musei di storia naturale. Uno di essi, fra i più noti, il bolognese Aldrovandi definiva il suo lavoro *"teatro"*, o *"microcosmo di natura"*, egli mise a disposizione degli studiosi ben 18.000 *"diversità di cose naturali"* e 7.000 *"piante essiccate in quindici volumi"*. Della raccolta erano parte integrante i 17 volumi contenenti migliaia di splendidi acquerelli raffiguranti animali, piante, minerali e mostri... Questi rispondevano alla precisa consapevolezza dell'Aldrovandi e dei suoi colleghi del ruolo centrale, nell'ambito della ricerca, delle immagini che a loro parere erano infatti di grande utilità per la circolazione delle conoscenze, offrendo un ritratto fedele delle *"cose di natura"*.

www.ingramcontent.com/pod-product-compliance
Lightning Source LLC
Chambersburg PA
CBHW041242020426
42333CB00003B/54